This Journal belongs to

_____

_____

Thank You For

Date

Personal Challenges

People To Pray For

Society And Government

Reflections

Thank You For

Date

Personal Challenges

People To Pray For

Society And Government

Reflections

Thank You For

Date

People To Pray For

Personal Challenges

Society And Government

Reflections

Thank You For

_____
_____
_____
_____
_____

Date

_____

People To Pray For

_____
_____
_____
_____
_____
_____
_____
_____
_____

Personal Challenges

_____
_____
_____
_____
_____

Society And Government

_____
_____
_____
_____
_____

Reflections

_____
_____
_____
_____
_____

Thank You For

_____
_____
_____
_____
_____

Personal Challenges

_____
_____
_____
_____
_____

Society And Government

_____
_____
_____
_____
_____

Reflections

_____
_____
_____
_____
_____

Date

_____

People To Pray For

_____
_____
_____
_____
_____
_____
_____
_____
_____
_____
_____

Thank You For

Date

Personal Challenges

People To Pray For

Society And Government

Reflections

Thank You For

Date

People To Pray For

Personal Challenges

Society And Government

Reflections

Thank You For

_____
_____
_____
_____
_____

Personal Challenges

_____
_____
_____
_____
_____

Society And Government

_____
_____
_____
_____
_____

Date

_____

People To Pray For

_____
_____
_____
_____
_____
_____
_____
_____
_____
_____

Reflections

_____
_____
_____
_____
_____

Thank You For

_____
_____
_____
_____

Personal Challenges

_____
_____
_____
_____
_____

Society And Government

_____
_____
_____
_____

Reflections

_____
_____
_____
_____

Date

_____

People To Pray For

_____
_____
_____
_____
_____
_____
_____
_____

Thank You For

_____
_____
_____
_____
_____

Date

_____

People To Pray For

_____
_____
_____
_____
_____
_____
_____
_____
_____
_____

Personal Challenges

_____
_____
_____
_____
_____
_____

Society And Government

_____
_____
_____
_____
_____

Reflections

_____
_____
_____
_____
_____

Thank You For

Date

Personal Challenges

People To Pray For

Society And Government

Reflections

Thank You For

Date

Personal Challenges

People To Pray For

Society And Government

Reflections

Thank You For

_____
_____
_____
_____
_____

Personal Challenges

_____
_____
_____
_____
_____

Society And Government

_____
_____
_____
_____

Reflections

_____
_____
_____
_____
_____

Date

_____

People To Pray For

_____
_____
_____
_____
_____
_____
_____
_____
_____
_____

Thank You For

_____
_____
_____
_____

Date

_____

People To Pray For

_____
_____
_____
_____
_____
_____
_____
_____
_____
_____

Personal Challenges

_____
_____
_____
_____
_____

Society And Government

_____
_____
_____
_____
_____

Reflections

_____
_____
_____
_____
_____

Thank You For

Date

Personal Challenges

People To Pray For

Society And Government

Reflections

Thank You For

_____
_____
_____
_____
_____

Personal Challenges

_____
_____
_____
_____
_____

Society And Government

_____
_____
_____
_____
_____

Date

_____

People To Pray For

_____
_____
_____
_____
_____
_____
_____
_____
_____

Reflections

_____
_____
_____
_____
_____

Thank You For

Date

Personal Challenges

People To Pray For

Society And Government

Reflections

Thank You For

_____
_____
_____
_____
_____

Date

_____

People To Pray For

_____
_____
_____
_____
_____
_____
_____
_____
_____

Personal Challenges

_____
_____
_____
_____
_____

Society And Government

_____
_____
_____
_____
_____

Reflections

_____
_____
_____
_____
_____

Thank You For

Date

People To Pray For

Personal Challenges

Society And Government

Reflections

Thank You For

Date

People To Pray For

Personal Challenges

Society And Government

Reflections

Thank You For

Date

Personal Challenges

People To Pray For

Society And Government

Reflections

Thank You For

Date

People To Pray For

Personal Challenges

Society And Government

Reflections

Thank You For

Date

Personal Challenges

People To Pray For

Society And Government

Reflections

Thank You For

Date

People To Pray For

Personal Challenges

Society And Government

Reflections

Thank You For

_____
_____
_____
_____
_____

Personal Challenges

_____
_____
_____
_____
_____

Society And Government

_____
_____
_____
_____
_____

Reflections

_____
_____
_____
_____
_____

Date

_____

People To Pray For

_____
_____
_____
_____
_____
_____
_____
_____
_____
_____
_____
_____

Thank You For

Date

Personal Challenges

People To Pray For

Society And Government

Reflections

Thank You For

Date

Personal Challenges

People To Pray For

Society And Government

Reflections

Thank You For

_____
_____
_____
_____
_____

Personal Challenges

_____
_____
_____
_____
_____

Society And Government

_____
_____
_____
_____
_____

Reflections

_____
_____
_____
_____

Date

_____

People To Pray For

_____
_____
_____
_____
_____
_____
_____
_____
_____
_____

Thank You For

_____
_____
_____
_____
_____

Personal Challenges

_____
_____
_____
_____
_____

Society And Government

_____
_____
_____
_____
_____

Reflections

_____
_____
_____
_____

Date

_____

People To Pray For

_____
_____
_____
_____
_____
_____
_____
_____
_____
_____

Thank You For

Date

Personal Challenges

People To Pray For

Society And Government

Reflections

Thank You For

_____
_____
_____
_____
_____

Personal Challenges

_____
_____
_____
_____
_____

Society And Government

_____
_____
_____
_____
_____

Reflections

_____
_____
_____
_____
_____

Date

_____

People To Pray For

_____
_____
_____
_____
_____
_____
_____
_____
_____
_____
_____

Thank You For

_____
_____
_____
_____
_____

Personal Challenges

_____
_____
_____
_____
_____

Society And Government

_____
_____
_____
_____
_____

Date

_____

People To Pray For

_____
_____
_____
_____
_____
_____
_____
_____
_____
_____

Reflections

_____
_____
_____
_____
_____

Thank You For

Date

Personal Challenges

People To Pray For

Society And Government

Reflections

Thank You For

_____
_____
_____
_____
_____

Date

_____

Personal Challenges

_____
_____
_____
_____
_____

People To Pray For

_____
_____
_____
_____
_____
_____
_____
_____
_____

Society And Government

_____
_____
_____
_____
_____

Reflections

_____
_____
_____
_____
_____

Thank You For

Date

Personal Challenges

People To Pray For

Society And Government

Reflections

Thank You For

Date

Personal Challenges

People To Pray For

Society And Government

Reflections

Thank You For

_____
_____
_____
_____
_____

Personal Challenges

_____
_____
_____
_____
_____

Society And Government

_____
_____
_____
_____
_____

Reflections

_____
_____
_____
_____
_____

Date

_____

People To Pray For

_____
_____
_____
_____
_____
_____
_____
_____
_____
_____
_____

Thank You For

Date

Personal Challenges

People To Pray For

Society And Government

Reflections

Thank You For

Date

People To Pray For

Personal Challenges

Society And Government

Reflections

Thank You For

Date

People To Pray For

Personal Challenges

Society And Government

Reflections

Thank You For

Date

Personal Challenges

People To Pray For

Society And Government

Reflections

Thank You For

Date

People To Pray For

Personal Challenges

Society And Government

Reflections

Thank You For

Date

People To Pray For

Personal Challenges

Society And Government

Reflections

Thank You For

Date

Personal Challenges

People To Pray For

Society And Government

Reflections

Thank You For

_____
_____
_____
_____
_____

Personal Challenges

_____
_____
_____
_____
_____

Society And Government

_____
_____
_____
_____
_____

Reflections

_____
_____
_____
_____
_____

Date

_____

People To Pray For

_____
_____
_____
_____
_____
_____
_____
_____
_____
_____

Thank You For

Date

Personal Challenges

People To Pray For

Society And Government

Reflections

Thank You For

Date

Personal Challenges

People To Pray For

Society And Government

Reflections

Thank You For

Date

Personal Challenges

People To Pray For

Society And Government

Reflections

Thank You For

_____
_____
_____
_____
_____

Personal Challenges

_____
_____
_____
_____
_____

Society And Government

_____
_____
_____
_____
_____

Reflections

_____
_____
_____
_____
_____

Date

_____

People To Pray For

_____
_____
_____
_____
_____
_____
_____
_____
_____
_____

Thank You For

_____
_____
_____
_____

Date

_____

People To Pray For

_____
_____
_____
_____
_____
_____
_____
_____
_____
_____

Personal Challenges

_____
_____
_____
_____
_____

Society And Government

_____
_____
_____
_____
_____

Reflections

_____
_____
_____
_____
_____

Thank You For

Date

People To Pray For

Personal Challenges

Society And Government

Reflections

Thank You For

Date

People To Pray For

Personal Challenges

Society And Government

Reflections

Thank You For

_____
_____
_____
_____
_____

Personal Challenges

_____
_____
_____
_____
_____

Society And Government

_____
_____
_____
_____
_____

Reflections

_____
_____
_____
_____
_____

Date

_____

People To Pray For

_____
_____
_____
_____
_____
_____
_____
_____
_____

Thank You For

_____
_____
_____
_____
_____

Date

_____

People To Pray For

_____
_____
_____
_____
_____
_____
_____
_____
_____
_____
_____

Personal Challenges

_____
_____
_____
_____
_____

Society And Government

_____
_____
_____
_____
_____

Reflections

_____
_____
_____
_____
_____

Thank You For

_____
_____
_____
_____

Date

_____

People To Pray For

_____
_____
_____
_____

Personal Challenges

_____
_____
_____
_____
_____

_____
_____
_____
_____
_____

Society And Government

_____
_____
_____
_____

_____
_____
_____

Reflections

_____
_____
_____
_____

Thank You For

Date

People To Pray For

Personal Challenges

Society And Government

Reflections

Thank You For

_____
_____
_____
_____
_____

Personal Challenges

_____
_____
_____
_____
_____

Society And Government

_____
_____
_____
_____
_____

Reflections

_____
_____
_____
_____
_____

Date

_____

People To Pray For

_____
_____
_____
_____
_____
_____
_____
_____
_____
_____

Thank You For

_____
_____
_____
_____
_____

Date

_____

People To Pray For

_____
_____
_____
_____
_____
_____
_____
_____
_____
_____

Personal Challenges

_____
_____
_____
_____
_____

Society And Government

_____
_____
_____
_____
_____

Reflections

_____
_____
_____
_____

Thank You For
_____
_____
_____
_____
_____

Personal Challenges
_____
_____
_____
_____
_____

Society And Government
_____
_____
_____
_____
_____

Reflections
_____
_____
_____
_____
_____

Date
_____

People To Pray For
_____
_____
_____
_____
_____
_____
_____
_____
_____
_____

Thank You For

_____
_____
_____
_____
_____

Personal Challenges

_____
_____
_____
_____
_____

Society And Government

_____
_____
_____
_____
_____

Reflections

_____
_____
_____
_____
_____

Date

_____

People To Pray For

_____
_____
_____
_____
_____
_____
_____
_____
_____
_____

Thank You For

Date

People To Pray For

Personal Challenges

Society And Government

Reflections

Thank You For

Date

People To Pray For

Personal Challenges

Society And Government

Reflections

Thank You For

_____
_____
_____
_____
_____

Date

_____

People To Pray For

_____
_____
_____
_____
_____
_____
_____
_____
_____

Personal Challenges

_____
_____
_____
_____
_____

Society And Government

_____
_____
_____
_____

Reflections

_____
_____
_____
_____
_____

Thank You For

Date

Personal Challenges

People To Pray For

Society And Government

Reflections

Thank You For

Date

People To Pray For

Personal Challenges

Society And Government

Reflections

Thank You For

_____
_____
_____
_____
_____

Date

_____

People To Pray For

_____
_____
_____
_____
_____
_____
_____
_____
_____
_____
_____
_____

Personal Challenges

_____
_____
_____
_____
_____
_____

Society And Government

_____
_____
_____
_____
_____

Reflections

_____
_____
_____
_____
_____

Thank You For

Date

People To Pray For

Personal Challenges

Society And Government

Reflections

Thank You For

Date

People To Pray For

Personal Challenges

Society And Government

Reflections

Thank You For

_____
_____
_____
_____

Date

_____

People To Pray For

_____
_____
_____
_____
_____
_____
_____
_____
_____

Personal Challenges

_____
_____
_____
_____
_____

Society And Government

_____
_____
_____
_____
_____

Reflections

_____
_____
_____
_____
_____

Thank You For

Date

Personal Challenges

People To Pray For

Society And Government

Reflections

Thank You For

_____
_____
_____
_____
_____

Date

_____

People To Pray For

_____
_____
_____
_____
_____
_____
_____
_____
_____

Personal Challenges

_____
_____
_____
_____
_____

Society And Government

_____
_____
_____
_____

Reflections

_____
_____
_____
_____
_____

Thank You For

Date

Personal Challenges

People To Pray For

Society And Government

Reflections

Thank You For

Date

Personal Challenges

People To Pray For

Society And Government

Reflections

Thank You For

_____
_____
_____
_____
_____

Date

_____

People To Pray For

_____
_____
_____
_____
_____
_____
_____
_____
_____

Personal Challenges

_____
_____
_____
_____
_____

Society And Government

_____
_____
_____
_____
_____

Reflections

_____
_____
_____
_____
_____

Thank You For

Date

People To Pray For

Personal Challenges

Society And Government

Reflections

Thank You For

_____
_____
_____
_____
_____
_____

Personal Challenges

_____
_____
_____
_____
_____
_____

Society And Government

_____
_____
_____
_____
_____
_____

Date

_____

People To Pray For

_____
_____
_____
_____
_____
_____
_____
_____
_____
_____
_____
_____

Reflections

_____
_____
_____
_____
_____

Thank You For

_____
_____
_____
_____

Date

_____

People To Pray For

_____
_____
_____
_____
_____
_____
_____
_____
_____

Personal Challenges

_____
_____
_____
_____

Society And Government

_____
_____
_____
_____

Reflections

_____
_____
_____
_____

Thank You For

Date

People To Pray For

Personal Challenges

Society And Government

Reflections

Thank You For

Date

People To Pray For

Personal Challenges

Society And Government

Reflections

Thank You For

Date

People To Pray For

Personal Challenges

Society And Government

Reflections

Thank You For

Date

People To Pray For

Personal Challenges

Society And Government

Reflections

Thank You For

Date

People To Pray For

Personal Challenges

Society And Government

Reflections

Thank You For

Date

People To Pray For

Personal Challenges

Society And Government

Reflections

Thank You For

Date

Personal Challenges

People To Pray For

Society And Government

Reflections

Thank You For

_____
_____
_____
_____
_____

Personal Challenges

_____
_____
_____
_____
_____

Society And Government

_____
_____
_____
_____
_____

Reflections

_____
_____
_____
_____

Date

_____

People To Pray For

_____
_____
_____
_____
_____
_____
_____
_____
_____
_____
_____

Thank You For

Date

People To Pray For

Personal Challenges

Society And Government

Reflections

Thank You For

_____
_____
_____
_____
_____

Personal Challenges

_____
_____
_____
_____
_____

Society And Government

_____
_____
_____
_____
_____

Reflections

_____
_____
_____
_____
_____

Date

_____

People To Pray For

_____
_____
_____
_____
_____
_____
_____
_____
_____
_____
_____

Thank You For

Date

Personal Challenges

People To Pray For

Society And Government

Reflections

Thank You For

Date

People To Pray For

Personal Challenges

Society And Government

Reflections

Thank You For

_____
_____
_____
_____

Date

_____

People To Pray For

_____
_____
_____
_____
_____
_____
_____
_____
_____
_____

Personal Challenges

_____
_____
_____
_____
_____

Society And Government

_____
_____
_____
_____
_____

Reflections

_____
_____
_____
_____
_____

Thank You For

_____
_____
_____
_____
_____

Date

_____

People To Pray For

_____
_____
_____
_____
_____
_____
_____
_____
_____
_____

Personal Challenges

_____
_____
_____
_____
_____

Society And Government

_____
_____
_____
_____
_____

Reflections

_____
_____
_____
_____
_____

Thank You For

Date

Personal Challenges

People To Pray For

Society And Government

Reflections

Thank You For

_____
_____
_____
_____
_____

Personal Challenges

_____
_____
_____
_____
_____

Society And Government

_____
_____
_____
_____
_____

Reflections

_____
_____
_____
_____
_____

Date

_____

People To Pray For

_____
_____
_____
_____
_____
_____
_____
_____
_____
_____

Thank You For

_____
_____
_____
_____
_____

Personal Challenges

_____
_____
_____
_____
_____

Society And Government

_____
_____
_____
_____
_____

Date

_____

People To Pray For

_____
_____
_____
_____
_____
_____
_____
_____
_____
_____
_____

Reflections

_____
_____
_____
_____
_____

Thank You For

_____
_____
_____
_____

Date

_____

People To Pray For

_____
_____
_____
_____
_____
_____
_____
_____
_____
_____

Personal Challenges

_____
_____
_____
_____
_____

Society And Government

_____
_____
_____
_____
_____

Reflections

_____
_____
_____
_____
_____

Thank You For

Date

People To Pray For

Personal Challenges

Society And Government

Reflections

Thank You For

_____
_____
_____
_____

Date

_____

People To Pray For

_____
_____
_____
_____
_____
_____
_____
_____
_____

Personal Challenges

_____
_____
_____
_____

Society And Government

_____
_____
_____
_____
_____

Reflections

_____
_____
_____
_____
_____

Thank You For

_____
_____
_____
_____

Personal Challenges

_____
_____
_____
_____
_____

Society And Government

_____
_____
_____
_____
_____

Reflections

_____
_____
_____
_____

Date

_____

People To Pray For

_____
_____
_____
_____
_____
_____
_____
_____
_____
_____

Thank You For

_____
_____
_____
_____
_____

Personal Challenges

_____
_____
_____
_____
_____

Society And Government

_____
_____
_____
_____
_____

Reflections

_____
_____
_____
_____
_____

Date

_____

People To Pray For

_____
_____
_____
_____
_____
_____
_____
_____
_____
_____
_____

Made in the USA
Monee, IL
20 February 2022